Copyright

Copyright © 2018 by Paul A. Blake all rights reserved. No part of this work covered by the copyright herein may be reproduced or used in any form or by any means – graphic, electronic or mechanical – without prior permission of the author

40 Days to Abundant Living

A note from the author

40 Days to Abundant Living is more than just another self-help book full of promises. It is a book that indulges in the importance of how positive thinking and practical application impacts a life of success. 40 Days to Abundant living provides a daily paragraph of inspiring words drawn from various aspects of life. It gives the reader the opportunity to make commitments and set a realistic goal that will move them towards discovering passion and purpose. The foundation of this book is from the perspective of faith that works. Therefore a verse or two from the Bible is provided to remind the reader that in all things a great God is working in them and through them.

Challenge: Challenge yourself to live the abundant life.
Commitment: Commit to changing something on your journey.
Goal: Set yourself goals for abundant living.
Bible: Order your steps with reminders from God's word for abundant living.

All biblical references are from the New International Version of the Bible (NIV).

Contents

Day One - Integrity 3

Day Two - Dream it 4

Day Three - Transformation 5

Day Four - Belief 6

Day Five - Determination 7

Day Six - Shine bright 8

Day Seven - Trust 9

Day Eight - Laughter 10

Day Nine - Naked truth 11

Day Ten - Potential 12

Day Eleven - No easy street 13

Day Twelve - By example 14

Day Thirteen - Hard work 15

Day Fourteen - Education 16

Day Fifteen - Emancipation 17

Day Sixteen - Step by step 18

Day Seventeen - Give more 19

Day Eighteen - Life's lessons 20

Day Nineteen - Shared talents 21

Day Twenty - Step out 22

Day Twenty-One- Sweet Success ………………………….…… 23

Day Twenty-Two- Satisfaction …………………………....… 24

Day Twenty Three- Ambition ……………………………… 25

Day twenty Four- Investment …………………………….. 26

Day Twenty-Five- No fear …………………………………… 27

Day Twenty-Six- Book of Life ……………………………… 28

Day Twenty-Seven- Opportunities …………………...…… 29

Day Twenty-Eight- No limit ……………………………….. 30

Day Twenty-Nine- Greatness ………………………..…… 31

Day Thirty- Live purposefully …………………………… 32

Day Thirty-One- Desire …………………………………… 33

Day Thirty-Two- The journey …………………………… 34

Day Thirty-Three- Distractions ………………………… 35

Day Thirty Four- Pursuing passion …………………………… 36

Day Thirty-Five- Discovery ………………………………… 37

Day Thirty-Six- Today matters ………………………….. 38

Day Thirty-Seven- Circumstances ……………………………… 39

Day Thirty-Eight- In the shadow …………………….…… 40

Day Thirty-Nine- Pride …………………………………… 41

Day Forty- Percentage …………………………………… 42

Day One
Integrity

Integrity is the cornerstone upon which success is built.
"Shall you hold on to your integrity". These were the fateful words uttered by Job's wife in the darkness of his despair. Job's response to her is befitting "you speak as one of the foolish women do". Even in the depths of his suffering he just could not charge God for doing wrong. When we know, what is right it is difficult for us to do what is wrong and feel comfortable. Integrity is what will keep many of us from making the wrong choices as we strive for success. We should not sell ourselves short if we know what we are doing is right no matter the cost stick to doing it because integrity does pay rich dividends in the end.

A. Challenge
B. Commitment
C. Goal
D. Bible Verse

Proverbs 11: 3
The integrity of the upright guides them, but the unfaithful are destroyed by their duplicity.

Day Two
Dream it

Trust your instincts if you can dream it, it can be done, so pursuit it with all you've got.

Myles Monroe said, "the richest place on earth is the graveyard because many people die and have all their dreams buried with them". Most of the things that we dream about are things that can be done if we learn how to trust in our abilities. It is not difficult to dream about anything, but putting our dreams into action may the one obstacle that keeps standing in our way. If we can dream it, it is an indication that whatever it is can be done. If it can be done then we owe it to ourselves to pursue it with all the strength we have in our mortal frames. Even if we do not achieve it in this life, we would have succeeded in leaving a legacy for someone else to complete that which we have started.

A. Challenge
B. Commitment
C. Goal
D. Bible Verse

Jeremiah 29:11

'For I know the plans I have for you,' says the Lord. 'They are plans for good and not for disaster, to give you a future and a hope.

Day Three
Transformation

Diamonds are formed under extreme pressure. Think of yourself as a diamond in the rough waiting to be transformed.
You will never know the kind of strength you possess until you are under pressure. The ability to glisten like a diamond is the ultimate achievement for many in this world, but it is often forgotten how much a diamond must go through to proclaim its beauty. Have a willingness to be placed under extreme not once, but several times if success is what you desire. While you are being moulded and fashioned into a thing a beauty always remember that your transformation came at a cost. You had to be put through the fiery furnace to remove all that was useless so that you could glimmer in the splendour of success.

A. Challenge
B. Commitment
C. Goal
D. Bible Verse

1Peter 1: 7
These have come so that the proven genuineness of your faith--of greater worth than gold, which perishes even though refined by fire--may result in praise, glory and honour when Jesus Christ is revealed.

Day Four
Belief

Believe in the potential that other people see in you.
It is interesting how easy it is for us to believe the negative things that people say about us, but almost impossible to accept when people speak positive words over our lives. Even if there are people that don't believe in your abilities there are a few who see the potential that is in you, no matter how deep it is buried. Pay attention when people speak positive words over your life. You may not know at first, but eventually, you will understand that they were on to something. The people in our lives are not always there to bring us down. There are those who will help to unlock our potential by speaking positive words over our lives.

A.   Challenge
B.   Commitment
C.   Goal
D.   Bible Verse

Ephesians 3: 20
Now to him who can do immeasurably more than all we ask or imagine, according to his power that is at work within us.

Day Five
Determination

A determined spirit is the most priceless treasure you can find while mining for success.

What we put into life is what we get out of it. Being successful requires an attitude of determination that refuses to accept defeat. It does not matter how many times we must start over because of failure, that is just the way life is, and we are not that unique. Finding our purpose will often demand that we have tunnel vision. We must keep focused and avoid distractions. We must be determined to pursue our hopes and dreams with passion and precision. Only then can we be satisfied that we have fulfilled our destiny.

- A. Challenge
- B. Commitment
- C. Goal
- D. Bible Verse

1 Corinthians 9:24-27

Do you not know that those who run in a race all run, but only one receives the prize? Run in such a way that you may win.

Day Six
Shine bright

You are not just another person in this vast universe you are a star meant to shine brightly for all to see.

Mediocrity is a curse to successful living. Our acceptance of the ordinary will keep us from taking a leap of faith to find our place in this world. You and I are not on earth to fill in space. We were created and put on this planet to make our mark and leave a legacy behind before we depart this life. We should not settle for a gravestone with two dates, when we were born and when we die. If one star does not shine at night that place, where it should have been, will receive nothing but darkness. If you and I do not live above the ordinary, the world will never have the privilege of seeing us shine.

A.   Challenge
B.   Commitment
C.   Goal
D.   Bible Verse

Philippians 4: 13
I can do all things through him who strengthens me.

Day Seven
Trust

Trust those who will tell you the truth no matter the cost.
The truth hurts, that is a fact, but it is the truth that eventually gives us wings to fly. Though the truth may be hard to absorb, especially when it comes from those we closest to us, it is worth it because this truth comes from the heart. The people who will tell us the truth about ourselves, no matter the consequences are worth keeping in our corners. They will allow us to examine ourselves with honesty and make the necessary adjust even if it makes us uncomfortable. Friends are hardly worth the investment if they are unwilling to expose our flaws, warts and all. The people who will tell us the truth and still be in the grandstand cheering us on are worth more than a pot of gold.

A. Challenge
B. Commitment
C. Goal
D. Bible Verse

John 8: 32
And you shall know the truth, and the truth shall set you free.

Day Eight
Laughter

Laughter makes the difficult days easier to bear.
Laughter is one of those simple things in life that can make any situation no matter how severe fade into nothingness. It is sad that it is the one thing that we don't do enough. We spend so much of our precious time chasing after things that don't matter that we forget that there is still much beauty in the world that deserves our smile. Our laughter conveys the messages that our hearts want to tell those whom we care about. It touches the soul in a way that words will never satisfy, laughter is worth a thousand words. Laugh often and let the world know it cannot move you. No matter difficult life gets there is always something to laugh about.

A. Challenge
B. Commitment
C. Goal
D. Bible Verse

Job 8:21
"He will yet fill your mouth with laughter, and your lips with shouting.

Day Nine
Naked truth

Don't get caught wearing the Emperor's new clothes.
The Emperor's New Clothes by Hans Christian Anderson is worth reading (read it please). The moral of the story is that when we play blind to what is happening around us, there is that one person brave enough to tell us the truth even when it is uncomfortable. Never settle for having people around you who will only appease your ego, instead embrace those who will tell you the hard truth and still surround you with love. The Emperor's New Clothes may look good in our minds, but it is important to remember that we are the only one seeing them.

A.   Challenge
B.   Commitment
C.   Goal
D.   Bible Verse

Isaiah 5:21
Woe to those who are wise in their own eyes and clever in their own sight.

Day Ten
Potential

You are a powerhouse of potential don't limit yourself by dreaming small. Though it is true that you must set yourself realistic goals limiting yourself to just the ordinary will not help you to achieve much. If you can dream of just anything why should you then settle for small dreams? When you can give yourself the room dream big, it offers you the opportunity to expand your territory. If you can only muster up the energy to have small ideas where is the excitement in that? Dream of doing great things that will leave your soul restless until the mission has been accomplished. Most people in this world that have left their mark in history were willing to take on tasks that were much bigger than themselves, you and I are no different. If you have the potential to dream, don't find satisfaction in imagining anything small.

A. Challenge
B. Commitment
C. Goal
D. Bible Verse

Psalm 139: 13-16

For you formed my inward parts; you knitted me together in my mother's womb. I praise you, for I am fearfully and wonderfully made. Wonderful are your works; my soul knows it very well. My frame was not hidden from you, when I was being made in secret, intricately woven in the depths of the earth. Your eyes saw my unformed substance; in your book were written, every one of them, the days that were formed for me, when yet there was none of them.

Day Eleven
No easy street

If success was easy, then all of us would be residents of Easy Street. Working towards success is not an easy task. Those who have had success had to work very hard to achieve it. Nothing that is worthwhile comes easy; to reap the fruits of your labour, you must be willing to put in the long hours that are required. Most people want to succeed, but few are prepared to take on the challenge or risk to make it happen. If success is your goal prepare to face numerous obstacles and you will have to decide what you are going to do with them. Success was not meant to be easy because only a few people would appreciate the value of hard work.

A. Challenge
B. Commitment
C. Goal
D. Bible Verse

Ecclesiastes 11: 6

In the morning sow your seed, and at evening withhold not your hand, for you do not know which will prosper, this or that, or whether both alike will be good.

Day Twelve
By example

Though the ant is one the smallest of earth's creatures, yet with its work ethic, it continues to move mountains. Learn from its example.

The ant is an industrious creature it is always on the move looking for something to do. Its small size does not stop it from taking on the greatest of tasks, a lesson worth learning. Anything that is worth doing is worth doing well; the ant does not think of the magnitude of the job it must do, it just does it. A healthy attitude towards work is among the first steps to having a successful life. The ant works tirelessly despite the elements because it understands the value of preparation. Whatever task you decide to undertake to make sure you commit to seeing it through to the end.

A. Challenge
B. Commitment
C. Goal
D. Bible verse:

Proverbs 6: 6-8

Take a lesson from the ants, you lazybones. Learn from their ways and become wise! Though they have no prince or governor or ruler to make them work, they labour hard all summer, gathering food for the winter.

Day Thirteen
Hard work

The only substitute for hard work is more hard work.
Hard work knows no limit; it finds little satisfaction in any task reaching completion. There no shortcuts or substitutes, the only option is to put in the time and effort required to get the job done. Hard work does not take success or achievement for granted, but will continuously seek new opportunities to improve on what was accomplished. It does not become frustrated with failure or setbacks. Instead, it taps into all the strength it can muster to try again and again until the objective has been reached. There is no substitute for hard work because it is where it all begins.

- A.   Challenge
- B.   Commitment
- C.   Goal
- D.   Bible Verse

Proverbs 14: 23
All hard work brings a profit, but mere talk leads only to poverty.

Day Fourteen
Education

Education helps us to see the world as it was meant to be seen by all. Education begins as a thirst for knowledge, but it does not end there. Education is not just a matter of acquiring knowledge of any subject, profession or career but also about being able to make the application of how this newfound experience relates to the world. This world is a place of unlimited potential, and the wisdom and knowledge we gain will help us to tap into our passion and purpose. Don't take being educated for granted; it is a privilege to see the world as you do, there is so much more to learn when wisdom and knowledge are your friends.

A.   Challenge
B.   Commitment
C.   Goal
D.   Bible Verse

Proverbs 1: 7
The fear of the LORD is the beginning of knowledge; Fools despise wisdom and instruction.

Day Fifteen
Emancipation

Emancipating yourself from the temptation to always thinking in the negative will drive you towards finding your purpose.
Separating yourself from the temptation of thinking negative things and the possibility of you finding your purpose will increase. What you think is what you will eventually become, therefore it is essential to make a conscious effort to take charge of your thought process. Negative thinking will not give you the courage to take on difficulties or believe that you can accomplish the impossible. Free yourself from negative thinking, and you will not only help yourself but image the countless others who will walk with you.

- A.   Challenge
- B.   Commitment
- C.   Goal
- D.   Bible Verse

Psalm 118: 5
I will walk about in freedom, for I have sought out your precepts.

Day Sixteen
Step by step

Wake up each day to the music of taking on the world one small step at a time.

One step at a time is all it requires to take your rightful place in this called life. It is not how fast or slow the pace you progress, but the fact that each step is bold and with purpose. Face life each day walking to the beat of your own drum, the world may play many tunes, but only your dance will matter. Step by step each mile is left behind until all that is before you is the reward of hard work and endurance. Each day brings with it the sound of music that is waiting for you to dance. Step by step you will find your rhythm only the journey matters not how well you sway to the melody. One step at a time wakes up to the music of taking on the world with passion and purpose.

A.   Challenge
B.   Commitment
C.   Goal
D.   Bible Verse

Ephesians 5: 19
Speaking to one another in psalms and hymns and spiritual songs, singing and making melody in your heart to the Lord.

Day Seventeen
Give more

Give more than you take and you will receive an abundance of opportunity. There is no harm in giving more than what is taken from life because the pay off is indeed worth it. Most people believe that if they are not always on the receiving end of life, there is not much to gain, but giving more often pays enormous dividends. Just about anyone can be a taker, it does not require much, but a giver who will make the sacrifice of extending way beyond what is necessary. Don't worry about it too much if you find yourself among the givers of this life, because life has a way of compensating you when it is least expected. If you are a giver, give all you got, hold nothing back because even if people abuse your kindness life will never forget who you are.

A.   Challenge
B.   Commitment
C.   Goal
D.   Bible Verse

Acts 20: 35

35 In everything I did, I showed you that by this kind of hard work we must help the weak, remembering the words the Lord Jesus himself said: 'It is more blessed to give than to receive.' "

Day Eighteen
Life's lessons

Each time you fail at anything file away the lessons learned to be used for future success.

Failure is not always a bad thing. Many lessons can be learned from failure that can be helpful on the journey towards successful living. Stop looking at every failure as a negative thing and begin looking for opportunities to learn something from them. If you fail and never gain knowledge, it is almost inevitable that you will be making the same mistakes many times. Each time you have to deal with failure instead of seeing as a stumbling block view it as a stepping stone on your way to discovering the abundant life. Keep your failures close to your heart, make them count by not repeating them. Use the lessons they have taught you as you continue to strive for the prize.

A.   Challenge
B.   Commitment
C.   Goal
D.   Bible Verse

Philippians 3:12
Not that I have already obtained all this, or have already arrived at my goal, but I press on to take hold of that for which Christ Jesus took hold of me.

Day Nineteen
Shared talents

Share your talents with the world selfishness will rob you of the joy of living. None of us is here to live only for ourselves. Most of us have at least one talent while others have several, but whether you have one or many they are all worth sharing. Sometimes the temptation to be selfish with our abilities can be overwhelming, but we stand to lose more than we gain living selfishly. Be willing to share your skills with as many people that are willing to learn from you it will always work out for your benefit. The joy of knowing that you have helped someone to realise their dreams because of what you have shared with them is soothing to the soul.

A. Challenge
B. Commitment
C. Goal
D. Bible Verse

Matthew 25: 28-29
"'So take the bag of gold from him and give it to the one who has ten bags. For whoever has will be given more, and they will have an abundance. Whoever does not have, even what they have will be taken from them.

Day Twenty
Step out

You don't belong in the shadows step out into the light of your purpose. You will gain nothing by hiding from success. You are as worthy as the people you admire every day of living a life full of purpose. Don't give anyone permission to treat any less than they would treat someone they consider important. The fact that you are alive in this moment of time is proof enough that you are here to do something great. Be willing to step outside of your inhibitions and become that tower of strength the world needs to know about. In the shadows is not where you belong because you were created to shine brightly so others can find their way.

A. Challenge
B. Commitment
C. Goal
D. Bible Verse

Matthew 5: 16
In the same way, let your light shine before others, that they may see your good deeds and glorify your Father in heaven.

Day Twenty-One
Sweet success

When the sweet taste of success is in your soul, it is difficult not to go searching for more opportunities.

Once you have experienced what it means to be successful, it is hard to let go of the feeling. Yes, working your way towards success can be very difficult and painful, but it worth almost every time. Most persons who experience success even once are not satisfied with just a taste; they go out seeking more opportunity to have that feeling linger as long as possible. If success is a disease it is worth catching and then spreading it far and wide, it is one of those things with which the soul cannot be satisfied. Strive To be successful and when you have found your worth making sure the feeling stays with you for as long as you can.

A. Challenge
B. Commitment
C. Goal
D. Bible Verse

Philippians 3: 14
14 I press on toward the goal to win the prize for which God has called me heavenward in Christ Jesus.

Day Twenty-Two
Satisfaction

The soul cannot be satisfied until passion and purpose have run their course. We are born to do something great. We should not be satisfied until we have discovered our purpose and pursued it passionately with all we have got to spare. There is no satisfaction to be found in living a mediocre life because we were designed for greatness. When we have departed from this earth, it must be said that we have lived life to the best way we know how. Live with passion and purpose because we only get to experience life just once. Step into your purpose and refuse to give in to the noise of detractors. Be passionate about discovering the greatness within you and refuse to die until you have reached your goal.

A. Challenge
B. Commitment
C. Goal
D. Bible Verse

Philippians 4: 8

8 Finally, brothers and sisters, whatever is true, whatever is noble, whatever is right, whatever is pure, whatever is lovely, whatever is admirable—if anything is excellent or praiseworthy—think about such things.

Day Twenty-Three
Ambition

Settling for less robs us of the ambition to pursue diligently what we deserve. Nobody deserves to settle for less than what they are truly worth. Settling for less will only lead us to live unsatisfactory lives. When we settle for just the minimum, we will not have the drive or ambition to maximise our potential. People who don't believe in us will try their very best to make us accepting of mediocrity, but it is our responsibility to know we are much more than we think we are. Settling does not give us the courage to take chances; it does not supply us with the energy that we require to take on life. To be more, we must first believe that we are worth more and be committed to diligently pursuing all that we know we deserve. Don't settle for less because settling will get you nowhere,

A. Challenge
B. Commitment
C. Goal
D. Bible Verse

Luke 12: 48

But the one who does not know and does things deserving punishment will be beaten with few blows. From everyone who has been given much, much will be demanded; and from the one who has been entrusted with much, much more will be asked.

Day Twenty-Four
Investment

Invest in those items that bring you peace of mind and a healthy appetite for living.

Life is an investment whatever dividends you gain is determined by the quality of what you invest and the time you spend investing. There is so much life we would like to have or experience, but in the end will all that we have gained be really worth it? If we are going to invest, then we may as well invest in the things that really matter. Most things in life are temporary; they are here only for a season eventually time will determine their worth. Make sure the items you invest in are worth the time and effort you spend on them. If you are going to invest in this life, invest in those things that will bring you peace of mind and a healthy appetite for living.

A. Challenge
B. Commitment
C. Goal
D. Bible Verse

Ecclesiastes 11: 6

Sow your seed in the morning, and at evening let your hands not be idle, for you do not know which will succeed, whether this or that, or whether both will do equally well.

Day Twenty-Five
No fear

Don't be afraid to take on a new challenge they help to build your character for future success.

Fear often keeps people from taking on new challenges. Most times they are satisfied with staying in the lanes that have been designated for them by people whose vision are limited. If doing just enough to get by is the best that we can do then we will know the magnitude of our potential. Life is about facing giants and obstacles, each challenge is an opportunity to change the world as we know it. If we accept the challenges of today, imagine how we would have shaped the world for tomorrow? Don't be afraid to take on doing new things every day, because you will never know where the journey may lead you.

A. Challenge
B. Commitment
C. Goal
D. Bible Verse

Isaiah 40:29
He gives strength to the weary and increases the power of the weak.

Day Twenty-Six
Book of Life

As you turn the page of life, history is being written that cannot be changed; turn the pages of your life with purpose.

We often think that because we are not rich or famous the contributions we make in life are insignificant. The truth is that everyone big or small is playing their part in writing history. As we contemplate on the many decisions, we have to make we should be reminded that our choices also affect the people around us. We are always in the process of writing history whether it is good or bad it is important to remember that what we write cannot be changed. Be sure that the account you are writing today is one that you and future generations can be proud of tomorrow. Be deliberate in writing your history, write it with purpose.

A. Challenge
B. Commitment
C. Goal
D. Bible Verse

Exodus 9:16
But I have raised you up for this very purpose, that I might show you my power and that my name might be proclaimed in all the earth.

Day Twenty-Seven
Opportunities

Don't wait for life to send you opportunities, grasp the moments, they are your opportunities.

Opportunity does not sit around the corner waiting for us to find it. Whatever we want out of life we are to go after it with determination. If we are comfortable just sitting and waiting for things to happen to us, we will be disappointed. Most of the times we have to be deliberate about making things happen. We have to create opportunities for ourselves if we are to be successful in life. Every moment we are alive, an opportunity will present itself, but we must be prepared to grasp it. We are to live anticipating that life will change in an instant, along with several opportunities we need to make use of. Don't wait for life to send you opportunities; grasp the moments, they are your opportunities.

A. Challenge
B. Commitment
C. Goal
D. Bible Verse

Romans 8:28

28 And we know that in all things God works for the good of those who love him, who[a] have been called according to his purpose.

Day Twenty-Eight
No limit

There is no limit to who I am and what I can accomplish because I am beautifully and wonderfully fashioned in His image.
I believe I was created in the image of a God who has no limitations. Therefore there is nothing in this world I cannot do. Whatever I put my mind to it can be accomplished I belong to Him. He placed on me the stamp of His approval and so it is my solemn duty to go and conquer the world. I will not rest until I am an accurate reflection of His unfailing love and compassion. I can do all things because His hand is what guides my decisions and order my steps. I will seek Him always because His promises have never failed. I am without limits or boundaries because I am beautifully and wonderfully fashioned in His glorious likeness.

A. Challenge
B. Commitment
C. Goal
D. Bible Verse

Genesis 1: 26-28

26 Then God said, "Let us make mankind in our image, in our likeness, so that they may rule over the fish in the sea and the birds in the sky, over the livestock and all the wild animals,[a] and over all the creatures that move along the ground."27 So God created mankind in his own image, in the image of God he created them; male and female he created them.

Day Twenty-Nine
Greatness

It does not matter what people think about you; greatness resides in what you believe about yourself.

People will think what they want to think of you whether or not you give them a reason to do so. No matter what people think about you, it is what you believe about yourself that is important. You can do little to change people's perception of who you are and that is really not your life's mission. Your path to greatness begins when you start seeing yourself in a favourable light. Don't allow what people think of you to control what you do with your life; you are the one who will suffer because of it. Life is too short to make what others think of you be what determines your destiny. Greatness begins with believing in yourself.

A. Challenge
B. Commitment
C. Goal
D. Bible Verse

2 Timothy 1:7
For the Spirit God gave us does not make us timid, but gives us power, love and self-discipline.

Day Thirty
Live purposefully

Life without purpose is a cursed existence that ought not to be tolerated. Living a purposeful life is intentional it does not happen by accident. To have a purpose it requires dreaming about things that even you sometimes are scared to accomplish. To have purpose is to have a mission that you intend to complete or you will otherwise die to try to finish. Purposeful living does not view life through a half-empty glass but instead sees the glass as forever half full. Without purpose, there is no challenge, nothing to look forward and everything to lose. No one should settle for a life without meaning because all human beings were created to experience much more than that. Life without purpose should not be tolerated.

A. Challenge
B. Commitment
C. Goal
D. Bible Verse

Ephesians 2:10
For we are God's handiwork, created in Christ Jesus to do good works, which God prepared in advance for us to do.

Day Thirty-One
Desire

Your purpose is driven by your desire to succeed; your desire to succeed is fueled by your ambition.

Success begins with a burning desire to achieve. This is also called finding purpose or meaning in your life. The desire to succeed makes the soul restless and thirsty until it has been satisfied. Success is fueled by ambition when an individual knows that they are alive to make a difference in this world there will be no peace to be found. Desire and ambition are like a consuming fire if it is not quenched with deliberate action. It will work in anyone's favour if they are suppressed. Desire and ambition are the two vehicles that transport the worthy passenger called purpose. When purpose has reached its destination, it will be welcomed into the open arms of success.

A. Challenge
B. Commitment
C. Goal
D. Bible verse

Jeremiah 1:5
Before I formed you in the womb I knew you before you were born I set you apart; I appointed you as a prophet to the nations.

Day Thirty-Two
The journey

Your journey to success may be arduous, but the taste of victory is sweet when you have finally reached your destination.

Whoever told you that success was an easy journey may not really know what success is. The road to success is often the road that few dare to travel on because most times it is paved over with difficult circumstances. It requires fortitude, patience and much longsuffering to realise the many dreams that you within you. Many times you will feel like giving up but always remember that it is not over until you have reached your final destination. After you have borne all the anguish and trying times the end result of struggles can only be the sweet taste of success.

A. Challenge
B. Commitment
C. Goal
D. Bible Verse

Romans 8: 37
No, in all these things we are more than conquerors through him who loved us.

Day Thirty-Three
Distractions

In spite of all that is happening around you avoid the distractions and keep focusing on the prize before you.

Distractions will keep you focused on the things that will not get you to your destination. Avoid paying attention to stuff in your life that has nothing to do with helping to get to where you want to go. You cannot always control life's circumstances, even with your best effort life can still be unpredictable. Focus on those things that add value to your life and what will help you to reach your goals. No athlete runs a good grace by always looking behind them they keep looking ahead because the prize is before them. Keep your eyes fixed on the things that matter most and forget about the stuff that you cannot change.

A. Challenge
B. Commitment
C. Goal
D. Bible verse

2Chronicles 15: 7
But as for you, be strong and do not give up, for your work will be rewarded."

Day Thirty-Four
Pursuing passion

As long as there is a single breath of life left in you pursue that which you are passionate about until you see it accomplished.

Live life deliberately, don't waste it chasing after meaningless ventures. Since we are given only one chance to live this life why not live it pursuing this thing that brings you real joy and being to your soul. What you desire may be challenging to accomplish but it worth it when you reap all the benefits. Refuse to have a spirit that gives up quickly anything worth having is worth the time you spend to gain it. Every day you wake up life is telling you that you have this moment to do something exceptional, believe it and live it. As long as there is breath in you pursue your dreams and aspire to greatness.

A.   Challenge
B.   Commitment
C.   Goal
D.   Bible verse

Isaiah 41: 10
So do not fear, for I am with you; do not be dismayed, for I am your God. I will strengthen you and help you; I will uphold you with my righteous right hand.

Day Thirty-Five
Discovery

You have not tried hard enough until you have discovered and fulfilled your purpose.

You may try your hand at many things in life, but do any of them have to do with finding and fulfilling your purpose. Life is not always about working harder but most times about working smarter. If you are going to work hard at anything, then give all the energy that you have to spare discovering your purpose and pursuing it with all the passion you can muster. This simple truth about life is what will bring you joy and allow you to live in the confidence that you have given your very best. If you are going to keep on trying at anything why not make it the thing that matters you the most? You must discover and fulfil your purpose.

A. Challenge
B. Commitment
C. Goal
D. Bible verse

Colossians 3: 23-24

Whatever you do, work at it with all your heart, as working for the Lord, not for human masters, 24 since you know that you will receive an inheritance from the Lord as a reward. It is the Lord Christ you are serving.

Day Thirty-Six
Today matters

Today only matters if we have lived it doing something worthwhile.
To live in the moment of each day is the goal of many people, but this is only worthwhile if it is spent doing something that makes a difference. Yesterday cannot be changed and tomorrow is uncertain, the only day that is really important is today. We can decide how we are going to live each moment of today, we can go chasing after clouds that have no value or we can commit to making each moment count for something. Today is full of promises and gifts waiting for you to unwrap and receive, every decision you make will either move you forward or make you look back with regret. Make each day count by doing something that will make a difference it is worth it.

A. Challenge
B. Commitment
C. Goal
D. Bible verse

Joshua 1:9
Have I not commanded you? Be strong and courageous. Do not be afraid; do not be discouraged, for the Lord your God will be with you wherever you go."

Day Thirty-Seven
Circumstances

Circumstances can either defeat you or bring you growth depending on the angle from which you view them.

The glass can either be half full or half empty depending on your perspective. Every negative situation can either make you or break you the choice is all yours. For everything that will happen to you-you can choose to grow and learn valuable lessons or you can decide to live in defeat. Life does not promise that things will always work out in your favour so don't live expecting it to. Live life being conscious that there will be some highs and lows, how you chose to handle them is what will make the difference. Though you may not be able to control what happens to you, what you do have control over is your response to life's situations. View life's circumstances from the viewpoint of always seeing the glass half full.

A. Challenge
B. Commitment
C. Goal
D. Bible verse

Proverbs 12: 24
Diligent hands will rule, but laziness ends in forced labor.

Day Thirty-Eight
In the shadow

Don't become a shadow of anyone, walk confidently in your own identity. Being a people pleaser is a sure way to live a miserable existence. Don't waste life seeking the approval of others because you will find yourself being disappointed a lot. Be comfortable with the knowledge that you always give your best effort at everything you do. If others don't approve of your efforts, you have absolutely nothing to lose. Being the best version of yourself is the most significant gift you can give to yourself. You are accountable to those who help you reach your goals. The people who love you don't need don't require you to walk in their shadow. They are quite happy with you being who you were born to be. Walk in confidence because it is your birthright.

A. Challenge
B. Commitment
C. Goal
D. Bible verse

Deuteronomy 31:6
Be strong and courageous. Do not be afraid or terrified because of them, for the Lord your God goes with you; he will never leave you nor forsake you."

Day Thirty-Nine
Pride

Take pride in the fruits of your labour, but don't celebrate so long that you forget there are other worlds out there to conquer.
Be proud of your hard work celebrate your success every opportunity you get. You have only one life to live, and nobody can appreciate the fruits of your labour as you can. Don't let people make you feel self-conscious about the hard work you have put in to get to where you are in life. But while you are celebrating remember that success is a journey with many destinations. Don't get distracted by yesterday's victory while tomorrow's adventure is yet to begin. Celebrate your past accomplishments but always remember that what lies ahead is yet to be discovered.

A.   Challenge
B.   Commitment
C.   Goal
D.   Bible verse

Psalm 16: 11
You make known to me the path of life; you will fill me with joy in your presence, with eternal pleasures at your right hand.

Day Forty
Percentage

Only about 7% of people in the world are born lucky, the rest will have to achieve everything through hard work and sacrifice.
Anybody who desires to experience success will not trust in luck as a dependable commodity. Those who spend valuable time depending on luck will find themselves being disappointed very often. There is no substitute for hard work; luck is an exception, not a rule to live by. Luck may find many people as they journey towards successful living, but never place all your confidence in being lucky. Commit to working hard, to working smart and to have a willingness to work through the places luck cannot reach. Lucky people will always be in the minority most people will have to work overtime to know the rewards of success.

A. Challenge
B. Commitment
C. Goal
D. Bible verse

Proverbs 12: 11
Those who work their land will have abundant food, but those who chase fantasies have no sense.

Professional Bio

Paul A. Blake is a vibrant and dynamic keynote speaker trained at the University of the West Indies, United Theological College, St. Michael's Theological College and the Jamaica School of Preaching and Biblical Studies. He believes in the power of decisive thinking in effecting change in the lives of all persons who have a desire to live an abundant life. He is a vibrant Jamaican man who has defied the odds and wants to share his incredible story of finding passion and purpose with the world.

Paul is CEO and Founder of Words Worthit Motivational Speaking and Training Co. Ltd a Faith-based company that specializes in helping people reach their heights of success through purposeful living. He believes that if people can change the way they think they can maximize their potential and go on to be passionate about life. Paul's story is one of resolve, strength and passion which has been shared locally and internationally on radio and television. He is frequently involved in giving motivational presentations and engaging in workshops at several organizations including companies, schools and other tertiary institutions.

He currently serves at the Independence City Church of Christ as their Associate Minister and is a Licensed Marriage Officer and Counsellor and the author of the motivational series Words to Inspire.

Paul is married to Racquel since 2007, and the union has produced one extra-ordinary son Timothy-Jordan, Paul's mantra is "I can do all things through Christ."

To connect with Paul visit his website at: wordstoinspireja.com, follow him on Instagram, LinkedIn and Facebook. For bookings contact wordstoinspireja.com

www.ingramcontent.com/pod-product-compliance
Lightning Source LLC
Chambersburg PA
CBHW072041060426
42449CB00010BA/2388